Mutiny Gallery

Winner of the 2011 T. S. Eliot Prize

The T. S. Eliot Prize for poetry is an annual award sponsored by Truman State University Press for the best unpublished book-length collection of poetry in English, in honor of T. S. Eliot's considerable intellectual and artistic legacy.

Judge for 2011: Tony Barnstone

For Jim & Darcy,
neighbors & friends,
with joy in
poetry,
Love Barbara
HVWC
12.11.11

MUTINY GALLERY

B. K. FISCHER

B.K. Fischer

New Odyssey Series
Truman State University Press
Kirksville, Missouri

Cover art: "A composite image of the 403 Highway in Hamilton," by Win Initiative. Courtesy of Getty Images.

Cover design: Teresa Wheeler

Library of Congress Cataloging-in-Publication Data

Fischer, B. K.
Mutiny gallery / B. K. Fischer.
        p. cm.
"Winner of the 2011 T. S. Eliot Prize."
ISBN 978-1-61248-011-4 (pbk. : alk. paper) — ISBN 978-1-61248-070-1 (ebook)
I. Title.
PS3606.I764M88 2011
811'.6—dc23

                                                                    2011026623

for John

Contents

Acknowledgments   ix

Paper House   1
Museum of Motion   3
Geographic Society   4
Motel Turkey   6
Museum of Miscellanea   7
Frog Fantasies Museum   8
Max's Down-to-Earth Rock Shop & Prehistoric Life Museum   10
Bread & Puppet Museum   11
Exotic World Burlesque Museum   12
Museum of Bad Art   14
Navajo Code Talkers Room   15
Church of One Tree   17
Hello Gorgeous Hair Museum   19
Museum of Menstruation   21
Musée Mécanique   23
House of Cash   25
Mon Bel Ami Wedding Chapel & Matrimony Museum   28
Clock & Watch Museum   29
Maidenform Museum   31
Killing Time Museum   33
Museum of Ordinary People   35
Archaeologist of Himself   37
Museum of Questionable Medical Devices   39
Max's Dreamland   40
Prayer Museum   41
Museum of Incandescent Lighting   42
Museum of Gems and Minerals   43
Museum of the Alphabet   46
Sensation Museum   47
American Diner Museum   49
House of Death   51
Max's Dreamland II   52
Restaurant Mutiny   53

Liars Hall of Fame   55
Pharmacy Museum   56
Carhenge   59
Home Sweet Home Museum   60
Wheels Through Time Museum   62
Paperweight Museum   63
American Precision Museum   65
Liquid Paper Museum   67
The End Is Near Museum   69
Museum of Papermaking   70
Museum of Museums   72
Honey of a Museum   73
First National Church of the Exquisite Panic   75
Prayer Museum II   77
The Lightning Field   79
Max's Dreamland III   81
Experimental Breeder Reactor #1   82
Next-to-Last Museum   83
Fall River House of Law & Disorder   85

Notes   89

About the Author   91

Acknowledgments

Grateful acknowledgment to the editors of *Ninth Letter,* where "Liars Hall of Fame" first appeared.

Many thanks to Jo Ann Clark, Troy Thibodeaux, and Jennifer Franklin for their faith and feedback during the writing of this book. I am also grateful to Tony Barnstone for offering vital suggestions, and to Nancy Rediger for seeing it into print. Much love and gratitude is due to James, Emily, and Lauren for their generous indifference to my typing, and for the windows their minds have opened on the worlds of childhood.

Paper House

Even the fireplace:
a cardstock flue,

linen-weave lintel,
structures of pulp.

A grandfather clock
cut from the dailies

of 48 state capitals,
a shoebox pedestal

to prop cartons
for a table, parcel

pillows, tissue sheers,
a chain of wrappers

to hang paper lanterns
across the corrugated

garden fence.
All origami décor.

Nothing she could not
crumple, crease, rip,

toss to the updraft
as confetti, fold in

an envelope. Nothing
she could not flatten

to fit in a carry-on
with a change of clothes,

one stuffed duffel
for the boy's briefs,

deck of cards, owl.
She pauses to find

prescriptions, birth
certificate, control.

Inside of an hour.
Then she crosses

the crêpe threshold,
lights a match.

Museum of Motion

Idling in the fire lane, she pulls him out
of school on Tuesday before lunch. Bears

right at the bank, merging with westbound
traffic as it nudges across the span toward

Rockland, a massive MTA Zamboni lifting
each slab of the barrier to make room

for rush hour the other way. Out of town,
out of reach of a thousand hourly acts:

stir, soak, sort, soothe, rinse, sign, stretch
another plastic liner over the pail, separate

paper and glass, compost the scraps.
Buy the right amount of milk to prevent

superfluous trips and spoilage. Out
of town, out of fear. No more minutes,

only miles, breaking it down into distance:
five, ten, fifty. Shot, jigger, fifth. Flare,

jack, spare. Make like a banana and. Like
a prom dress. She watches the rig close in

in the rearview, signals left. Left. She
tells him not to worry about forgetting

his spelling binder, permission slip, new
blue gloves. We're going for a drive.

Geographic Society

The map, upside down and backwards
in the windshield glare. When she tries
to refold it, Maine touches Orlando,

the Upper Peninsula overlaps Utah and
Kentucky accordions to Taos. Tosses it
into the trunk with the jumper cables.

He knocks the rearview mirror sideways
clambering over the seat to sit beside her,
studies the gunmetal river beneath twin

suspensions. Just buckle up with the strap
below your neck, duck if you see police,
God forbid a kid should get a clear look

at what's coming at him down the pike.
Then she frowns, slows and stops mid-
span, puts on hazards: a woman doubled

over the guardrail, hair covering her face.
Claire grabs some tissues, thinking the woman
must be getting sick. The woman turns her face

and it is shredded with fear. Claire offers
the tissue anyway. Rifles through her mind
for an inadequate scrap, something between

coercion and calm. The next place will be
better than the last place. I've got my son
in the car. The woman crouches, forehead

on the girder, lets the siren approach, lets
the trooper enclose her arms, lead her away.

Motel Turkey

They kick off their shoes, eat on the bed, out of reach
       of the crocodiles, steer their dream canoe
all the way to the Orinoco. He says, in my language
       the *Y* is always silent. A marshmallow counts
for less than a Cracker Jack peanut. She lets him
       dribble milk on the straw wrapper to see
the snake uncoil, watch raunchy cartoons, eat Cheez Whiz,
       stay up. He nibbles, asks: Who killed Jesus
and why did they do it? How does the blood
       come up to the cut? Go Fish, Crazy Eights,
War. Pick-Up Sticks, Countries, I Spy. I spy
       something with moving parts. I spy something
man-made. I spy something broken. Tomorrow
       they'll cross the desert, head west from here,
home of the king of western swing, population
       516. Tonight: 518. Just the two of them,
writing cowboy poetry until they get too tired.

Museum of Miscellanea

Woman with one of everything: dog,
        dogwood, Dormeyer mixer,
taxidermied checker-playing pair
        of possums, peck of oats, oars,
cotton gin, tinder box, matchbook, one-
        room schoolhouse, unassembled.
Shack, flat, hut—full to the tin roof
        with ambition: padlock, pet rock,
barbecue, birdbath, tie-rack, thumbtack,
        Midas tire, mailbox, knee-socks,
roasting pan, rotary phone, magazine,
        jellybean, Jesus action figure, jar.
Break it down by sound, row
        upon row, try to put a stop

to the sensation of sliding backwards
        the way a car at a light seems to roll
back when the one in the next lane pulls
        forward. Dog dies, grumpily,
at thirteen. Dogwood thins out
        but continues to bloom. No one

in that town has a stained-glass unicorn
        with a suction cup to stick it
to the pane. She must exchange her life,
        take it back, get credit, get a grip,
get mopping—breasts bobbing in the tank top
        like eggs in a pouch. She stands up,
gestures with one hand and a Sharpie marker—
        so, let me get this straight, is everything
A or is it *The*? Crayon, crossbow,
        crockpot, crow, crucifix, crutch.

Frog Fantasies Museum

They could live here forever
between land and water, toes

clinging to the underleaf, he,
suspended, splendid, in the stage

just past tadpole, sure of his legs
though the tail remains, she,

satisfied she has laid her eggs
on the model of bubbles,

clusters of froth, knowing
plasticine blues and greens

mean poison, the pulse
accelerates at the urging

of the hindbrain, not conscious
but alive, neither a memory

nor a prediction of the pith,
the formaldehyde, the novice's

clumsy scalpel bearing down
on the gel-filled underbelly.

Here, half asleep, breathing
the underwater light from

the Tropica Disco sign,
their skins cool to the touch.

At four fifteen an angry man
calls out from an upper story:

*Don't let me catch you
coming around here again.*

Max's Down-to-Earth Rock Shop
& Prehistoric Life Museum

A cache of shark teeth for luck in a Lucite box. Flint. Prisms. Pleistocene.
Mile markers every tenth of a mile, then every mile, then none. Red
balls strung on overhead wires to warn low-flying planes. Signs of the
Chinese zodiac. A stalagmite shaped like a fried egg. All the words to
the Beatles. Not mummies. Not mimes. Not the poop hatch in the suit of
armor. Constellations. Mammals of the Cretaceous. Infinity minus itself.
Not igneous: forged in fire but so full of air it could soak up tears. Not
sedimentary: something dead could slip in the sand through thousands
of years, turn up with its ancestors. Metamorphic: formed under intense
pressure, compressed fleck and crystal. His mother twisting her ring. Traces
of galactic lint. His mother showing him where the mouse had made a nest
in the cinderblock, a tunnel between two rooms. A thousand light years
away. His mother lobbing his father's glass against the wall. Shaved ice and
shards look the same in the dustpan. She wipes red dust off the windshield
and her sunglasses. Gust of mower exhaust and cut grass. License plate of a
Nissan: *je me souviens.*

Bread & Puppet Museum

He hangs his coat on the banister, tears the end off
the loaf and eats. Could she for once take the damn
wax paper off the butter before she puts it in the dish?
The oven mitt waves, takes a bow—Mr. Owl says
it's time for bed. Max comes into the kitchen, head
still wet from the bath, shirt tag showing in front.
Can't catch me I'm the Gingerbread Man. Eyes
his father's reddening brow, tie askew. Does
his boy want to learn a new defense in chess?
Smears the softened butter. Run run, mouseling,
Mr. Owl might have himself a nice micey pie.
Inhales himself taller at the ribcage, pushes
the single malt across the counter and away
from his father, who sets down the fork and knife
without a clink and strikes him across the mouth.

Exotic World Burlesque Museum

Dreams she is naked with a lover but can't
find a place to be alone—a hotel room laden
with noisy sleepers, a sliding door opening

at an intersection, a wall dissolving into
a department store where she crouches
among the racks, grabbing something

to cover herself. On the way out of Reno
the broken neon sign for Topless Go Go
flashes *less, less*. She stops for gas,

looks at the relics in the glass case under
rhinestone tags with each *nom de commerce*—
Daisy Constance Rae—accoutrements

of distraction, picked up in the bargain
bin with remnants of a paycheck: flip-
flops, lip-gloss, faux crocodile clutch.

She lights a cigarette, her first since
she snuffed out her sworn last
by the wheel of his stroller outside

a bodega in November 2001, the same
day she saw Osama bin Laden through
a cellar door on Dyckman Avenue.

Surely a seedy love scene is coming up,
a cheap fling, except she is traveling
with a chaperone too young to leave.

She fingers a key ring, only free
to take a peep, a body broken down
into boxes: ridge of a foot, glans.

Museum of Bad Art

God she was good. Post-Catholic-Marxist-feminist collagist,
she took an off-cast dishwasher and turned it into a tabernacle

with supermarket citronella saints (near the mouse traps), hung
rosaries off a lava lamp and devised a chapel from slivers

of Scotch tape. The jury found the results *ephemeral, fraught
with an irritable tenacity*, doled out the usual kudos and half-

tuition remission. Take your chances with the big city, take
this ticket out of Gambrills, where all there is, is a divided

highway with a median-strip Taco Bell and a sand quarry.
She wrote the requisite 17 pages on the last comma in Kafka,

plumped up the portfolio with a lobster-trap confessional,
a dot-to-dot triptych in Lite Brites, a multimedia installation

with Kierkegaard quotations to the tune of "Karma Chameleon."
She wanted to talk about kitsch and the str(i/u)ctures of faith,

blue-collar hallelujah bathos in a cross-stitched serenity prayer,
but her advisor leveled his gaze at her chest throughout the defense.

Too bad about those other girls, such promise but they turned out
to be bourgeois opt-out sell-out suburbanite incubators come home

to roost and lost their edge. That won't happen to you, will it?
Honey, you could light out for a dune in New Mexico, erect

a monumental neo-ziggurat topped with a fourteen-foot faun
wielding a pitchfork. You can't say trident—this is America.

Navajo Code Talkers Room

She tells people dad is dead,
        wrapped around a tree,
as if the metal tonnage

        crumpled like a plastic
wrapper between the moment
        of the wreck and when.

When are you going to
        check out? Why does he
keep looking at me like that?

        A tough nut to.
Under the pressure. Check
        the tire pressure.

Gas is on the rise.
        She picks up a pay-
as-you-go cellphone

        in Oklahoma and by
the time they reach
        Arizona there are

several holes in the plot.
        She squints at the replica,
frame and glyph, wishes

        her words were intricate
as those the Navajo set up
        to stymie the Japanese.

Elaborate cipher, tone. Get
       the gist. 400 men
so valuable to the war effort

      each had a personal
bodyguard. As if they carried
      the tricky glitches

of victory within them, as if,
      susceptible to capture,
their bodies exposed

      a soft muscle that might
be made to talk, as if
      they had any say.

Church of One Tree

It is late afternoon when they arrive at the Church of One Tree, get out and stretch. They have averaged 400 miles a day. The brochure says a century has passed since the good people of Santa Rosa set out to build a church from the timber of a single redwood

and a year since they rearranged it to pay homage to the itinerant Robert Leroy Ripley, a memorial to his birthplace. His suitcase, stickered-over, heavy-latched. Photographs of the amazements—two-headed calf, fur-bearing trout. Or not.

Claire is the only one in the museum. Max has run off to the bottom of a hill to poke around in some rocks. A rotating fan pushes a cabin smell across and past her, across and past. Folding chairs stacked against one wall suggest that perhaps the room is still used for a congregation or at least a group.

In the back alcove—sanctuary—there's art of a sort: cigar-box dioramas, folk engravings, driftwood furniture. She looks around

for something to make of it other than the usual cubist death riff, the cut-and-paste collage of what's left after breakfast, when a guitar becomes a side table with a water glass that sweats its sonorous hole.

Believe it: fastest snail, biggest litter, most pins in a scalp. *Not* is easy. She's already lost faith in everything from love to the postal service, from *the kingdom of heaven is within you* to the kingdom of heaven is within *y'all*, and still

without reason or incitement, finds herself believing with the ragged force of renunciation, the *anyway* dangling off the *I believe*.

The woman at the desk comes over to tell her they are about to close.

Max crashes in, amped up with exhaustion. Someone is trying to steal their car. She doubts it.

He grins, lifts up a picture on its wire to see what's behind it, picks at a sticker curling up on the famous valise. The woman closing up doesn't seem to care. Claire falls back

on it once again, the ornery old notion—a perfect skepticism questions disbelief. Believing

the last thing she believed the last time she believed the last thing she believed, she

gets her son in a headlock and gets their show on the road.

Hello Gorgeous Hair Museum

At the Venn intersection of Barbra Streisand
and Lolita, *libidreaming, lotioning,* she looks

herself in the eye. That she isn't prettier
is her long-standing grudge with God. Boy

with his long femurs, downy thighs, mouth.
When he is sullen like this, she talks to him

with the nervous and exaggerated politeness
of driving with a cop in view, the whole way

to French Lick, Indiana, 105 miles southwest
of Indianapolis, where the Wave-o-Matic

sits like a badger trap beside the penitential
straps of a primitive perm machine. She is

hoarse—her exasperation coarsening even
the clement phrase—smoking as she waits

for him to come back and kiss her
with perfunctory gratitude for a new pack

of Japanese cards. His hair: straw, so thick
the water she pours won't wet the scalp,

thick in her fist as she berates him, only
an instant until she acquiesces, eases into

endearment, offers a sweet, a song, a tale
to appease him as he resists, tires of this

thousand-mile stretch of silk-smooth road.

Museum of Menstruation

A visit with Aunt Ruby at the Red Roof Inn,
        planting cotton, strumming a banjo
in Sergeant Zygote's ragtime band,
        clogging Molly, Kitty's nosebleed,
medium rare, red thread in the sewing machine,
        Cousin Claudia's barbecue, Moses' parting,
Dracula's teabag, wound of Eve, up on blocks,
        the Cardinal's tomato boat, taking Carrie
to the prom, time to reboot, high time for high tide
        tide Tide tide Tide tide Tide.

He says, What's that pink thing behind the toilet?
        Trash. What's it for? Ladies.

A metaphysics of absorption: what comes
        between the drop and the diffusion,
the missed made manifest, potential blue.
        What if the one full moon had never
ripened, the one error never slipped,
        traveled its telescopic distance,

caught hold, caught in her? Become him.
        Would she be free? He picks up
and scrutinizes the ribbings, fitted tubes,
        perforated meshes, adhesive tabs,
cardboard cylinders, loosened strings,
        cotton batting full of white beads
of diaper gel. The biology book said

        the egg was the size of a period
on a page. Finitude and pause. A point

of dried ink, a fixed mark to curtail
the undulant energies of pitch and syntax,
dropped into the ocean of herself.

Musée Mécanique

All afternoon he puts together mechanical bodies,
sets a spine on its limbs, swivels an ankle, adjusts
a wing or talon. Later he wanders mildewed rooms

with fake grass and felt, toothpick amusements,
all the sorry promises of fortune-telling, binocular
vistas, boxed panoramas, swept-up peanut shells.

He knows how to make an axel spin a wheel.
Admires elegant contraptions, entrapments,
the shields and weapons added last—blade, bow.

A shutter dilates, snaps and contracts: a room
with a new machine, *l'enfant carburateur.*
It's schematic for sex he supposes—the same

piece missing between the spring and screw
he loses when he overhears adult conversation.
He knows how heavy those weights would be

on a hand, how cold—a long-legged boy, a boy
with a body like a racing Claudel, the metal shaft
and piston traced on vellum in pencil and gold,

running, running, running along the old pier,
weaving among the benches and vaulting stiles.
When the sun goes down on the bay he sets out

to run, to listen to himself run. He tries to disrupt
the rhythm, to syncopate his strides against the boards,
pauses and alters, hangs back to feel the almost

imperceptible fall in each step. He runs—rote
and rotor, turn of time, repeating as best he can his
known cadences, his staggered series of arrested falls.

House of Cash

Insufficient funds. Clams
fur wampum rice nugget coin.

A flattened piece of tin
with its imprint rubbed off.
A face seen only when the bill

is held to the light. Devices
to thwart numismatic ploys.

She maxes out the cash, runs
through what's liquid quick—
frozen, dried up, denied.

The boy is always hungry.
She stands too long in 7-Eleven

deciding on Fritos for lunch
over the five-dollar granola.
Temps are needed to spoon

food samples at the Price Club.
She mans a Bunsen burner,

offering tablespoons of Honey
Baked Beans in lined-up mini
soufflé cups. For nine hours.

Counts cups, staggers cups
in patterns, thinks she could

make them into snowdrops
or a pulp from which to sculpt
a bust of John the Baptist.

Pilfers some nuts, vanilla extract.
Five parts of fried chicken:

breast, thigh, keel, drumstick,
wing. Puts twelve boxes of
timecards in alphabetical order.

Capital *T*. Capital *A*. Capital
X. Are you filing jointly or?

Each stint, the kid's a problem:
no school bus, no Y. She
enlists the teenage hostess

on the cheap, returns to find her
smoking hash by the pool while

he pushes a skimmer to gather
fallen leaves on the surface.
Dropped on the concrete deck

behind the lounge chair is a
glycine capsule in a Ziploc.

He hates, *hates*, the old lady
with mustache and Sudoku
she met at the laundromat.

Next day, late, near broke:
just stay in the room. Read.

Keep the deadbolt on. All
roads lead to a diaper wipe,
a supply closet with bedpans.

Over, under the table, no job
that requires giving notice,

out of reach of direct deposit
and his arm, flung heavy as gold
over her chest while he slept.

Mon Bel Ami Wedding Chapel
& Matrimony Museum

Sixty miles outside Vegas, the song catches a static patch, a node in the power grid, interference from underground missile silos. Memory like the cedar astringency of aftershave. She accelerates, the broken yellow line shifting to the other side of the solid as she takes the curve. A man takes a call, an aspirin, a long step to clear the threshold, pushes off his muddy boots without his hands. Promises, promises. The guardrail shows signs of impact in several spots. A man hacks away at the overgrown hedge. Power lines, up ahead on the plateau. He'll never find us if we keep moving. A man picks up his son, awkwardly and only when asked. Outskirts now, double lines all the way. The son, bare feet on the dash: hale, pensive, disinclined to prattle. Not a trace of vapor in the air. A man speeds up the Saw Mill Parkway in slick weather, no shoulder, so much standing water she senses the hydroplane half a dozen times. When they arrive in one piece—two pieces—she weeps in the driveway. Goes in, finds him asleep in his shoes. A needle-width below empty. She pulls off the highway, fills up with regular while the boy picks out a comic and a pack of Pez. Power lines converge on a transformer. A man twitches his pen against his cheek. From the lawn of the real-estate office across the street comes a gust of mower exhaust and sagebrush. A man sips his wine, a syllabic caress of an old Bordeaux—black fruit, graphite, sweet tobacco. She leans in to breathe it—bruised apples, pencil shavings, soot.

Clock & Watch Museum

The virulent boredom of childhood:
counting ceiling tiles, streetlights,

things that begin with the letter *C*.
Waiting for the grown-ups to groom,

to pay, for the priest to say *go in peace*,
the rote and drag of the kneeling prayer,

scratching a fingernail in the grime
on the pew-back, gripped by so many

hands as they let themselves down.
The temptation to write on oneself.

To jiggle whatever body part is free
until told to stop, to bite whatever part

of oneself is dead until told to stop.
Copying the words. Writing sentences

with the words, drawing a diagram
of the parts and sums. More sums.

Counties, capitals, colons. Algebra—
the answers dive under the signs.

Pretending to read for the requisite
minutes, watching the colon after

the hour flash off on   :   :   :   :   :   :
punching in 55378008 and inverting

it BOOBLESS. Dividing the margin
into sixteenths, then coloring each block

of time as the class period elapses.
Waiting for the nurse, waiting for

the doctor to come in, jab the swab
in the throat. Doodling intricate

mechanisms, cogs, initials, one's
own name into strangeness, sleepy,

sure the name itself has changed,
looking up only to be called on again.

Maidenform Museum

Downstairs there's a Dr. Pepper machine
and an unplugged Ms. Pac-Man. A girl
about his age—a little older—comes in, says

her name is Christina except she changed
both *Is* to *Ys*. Her dad is a stuntman. If
you go from the pool to the hot tub too fast

you can die from blood boiling. She starts
to strip, arms in one at a time then disengages
her head. Her breasts aren't like his mother's,

which hang away from her body, but puffy
and beige like the round Band-Aids they put
over the spot of a measles shot. She folds

her bra, cup to cup. You have to learn to
undo it with one hand. He sneezes. She snaps
the swimsuit over her shoulders. What are you

looking at? Upstairs his mother, irritable,
drops her bra to the floor. Patent 1927.
Ginghams, gossamers, missiles, snowcones,

push-ups, second skins. I Dreamed I Was.
I Can't Believe It's Not Butter. Old fleshy duo,
once so admired by a lover he named them

Coconut and Key Lime Pie. Or maybe everyone
has a lover who does this. Afterwards: enormous,
ovoid as a pigskin and slick with lanolin, nipples

raw, his infant fist jerking to find the edge
of her nightgown, an underthing to grip as he
drew his milk—resolute pulls from the jaw.

Killing Time Museum

Keep the deadbolt on.
           She tells him about a story she read
in the paper about a two-year-old girl at a hotel who
bolted herself inside the room when her mother went
a few paces to the ice machine, and then could not
unlatch the lock, despite the mother's entreaties
through the door. The girl wiggled her fingers
under the jamb. He is unsure

           what point he's to glean from this.

Finally she leaves.
           First he lies on the bed, imagines
a duel between the murderer of sleep and the murderer
of time. Eats Cheez-Its and a banana, makes mosaics
from torn bits of newspaper circulars, recalls the phase
when he was five and ripped things during tantrums.
She's already stopped making him keep a log.

           The first west
swelled like the dorsal hump of a whale:
Appalachian Blue Ridge. I-81 past Mauzy,
Virginia, bridges like bandages over the road.
At Natural Bridge, he slunk behind the billboard
and trotted down sixty steps before the ticket-taker
sent him back up, short by $7 to see the arch.

           He thinks about
the Alamo and what would have happened had it
never been avenged. No state of Texas, the USA
a thinner-bellied creature with Louisiana and Florida
as its two front paws.

                    He is afraid
to go out but goes out. Takes the key. Mad dash
from the parking lot to the corner, then across
the tracks. On the busier street there's Rite Aid,
WaWa, Sunoco, IHOP, Kentucky Fried Chicken,
Hess. Down the end—pool hall, pawn shop, dry
cleaner, spiritual adviser.

                    No one talks to him nor
tries to stuff him in a trunk. Last year in the news
two boys had been found captive, abused—one
had been missing for four days, the other four years.
The older boy was sure he would be killed now that
the new kid had arrived.

                    He imagines them
splitting a package of crackers. Or picking at
the foam showing through the couch cushions.

                    He loses track
of time and panics, hops out to the median but then
has to wait for a long freight to pass. His eyes click
past each C, N, Canadian National boxcars, scrap bins,
raw lumber on a flatbed, then a run of maroon Central
Vermonts, same strokes in the logo under graffiti loops
LOBOS CATFISH I LOVE YOU IRIS JUNE

                    When he makes it back,

forty-one minutes have elapsed. He closes his eyes,
thinks about tonight when they will drive again,
when he will slip asleep as she drives through rain
and dark—the swoosh-eek, swoosh-eek of the wipers,
droplets like tadpoles squiggling down the glass,
illuminated red by running lights as the truckers pass.

34

Museum of Ordinary People

So that's the cliché she was living—the spectre
seems to sit beside her in the fun-house ride,

her own image reflected in the ornate frame.
One un-self-portrait after another, through the pane

of the car window while turning at a traffic light,
shoulder-checking, sliding into an angle slot

or handing over the cash at the drive-thru. Woman,
Band-Aids showing above the heels of her pumps,

her clutch half open. Woman combing, re-combing
white wisps over her pink scalp. Scrub nurse

with gray pigtails. Various twists to keep hair
off the back of the neck. Androgynous bus driver—

shaved head, hairless arms tattooed with vines, Kali
on a throne. Grandmother with pinch-faced toddler

in glasses, red strap to secure them. Paunches
that could have babies in them or not. Characters

in nobody's book, not even her own, as if she had
the time or the wherewithal to write it, call it

Sandpaper for the Soul, Ramen Noodle for the Ego.
Or even to scrounge around for a rectangular frame

at a tag sale, scour out the old gilt and insert her own
or her mother's or her child's retouched image where

the long-dead stranger was. Exhibit A, Exhibit One,
hung in a museum where the people never come.

Archaeologist of Himself

Homesick, carsick, he lines up his tools
for the operation: pipe cleaner, spy decoder,
floss. To excise, devise a method, divide

Lost from Found. He draws a diagram,
calls it "The Scratches of Marduke," realizes
he needs, is lacking, tape. After he peels
a strip of callous off the pad of his thumb,

the fingerprint remains. Wonders what
has become of his room, knows nobody
is ever going to dig it up under layers of ash,
mull over the meanings of the findings:
solar system Styrofoam, participation trophies,

a Strega Nona puppet on a popsicle stick.
Nobody did the summer reading. What if
he made up his mind, refused to move,
stood locked at the door. He didn't want to.
He wouldn't like it. He wasn't going.
Moving was just more waiting, sitting and

waiting for the wheels to stop. Going was
waiting. Resigns himself to another round
of Memory Dig, trawls his mind for something
he has never remembered before. Recent past
was cheating—what he just ate for lunch, or
the exit sign with the name of a town some
miles off. Tries first grade, not the teacher

but the glue tray, the smell of the coat alcove.
The Irish-Spring green of the tile in his grand-

mother's bathroom, before she died. As soon
as it starts to look familiar he has to stop,
switch, excavate another lode. Look under
the slide. In his father's toiletry kit. Water
with weeds in it, a peacock coming closer
and closer as he screams and grabs her leg.

Museum of Questionable Medical Devices

Bellyache: she warned him about the third doughnut
and now it has happened. Or maybe it was the fries
in vinegar and Old Bay, soft-serve vanilla, the smell
from the mini-golf lake run dry. He senses the jets
of saliva in the sides of his mouth before he heaves.

For a moment better. The TV spokesman explains
you'll be younger, more supple, better endowed.
She wipes his clammy brow, murmurs baby stuff
but sighs in a way he knows she's annoyed. Call
now, six-month supply for only. Nausea swells

again and the room contracts to the pattern
in the carpet, berber under a finger, faux-grain
of the head-board, pocks in the dropped ceiling.
Four screws in the metal plate affix the edge
of the wall-to-wall. A popcorn bucket serves

well enough. And absolutely free, get a second
deluxe set of magnets for your mattress and insoles.
Major credit cards accepted. Natty tropicana print
above his head, hibiscus and mildew, tub daisies.
She lays her hand over his eyes to urge them closed,

warms her always-cold hands on his fevered head.
His mother's hands—smelling of the vanilla extract
she rubs in to mask the odor of garlic or fish or vomit
or shit or whatever it is she has to handle that day.

Max's Dreamland

He dreams his father's scarf
wraps his neck too tight but
then wakes and realizes
he is wheezing. Reaches

for the inhaler's bitter puff.
Works on a loose back tooth.
Says his things to himself
to get back to sleep,

back to cities that skew,
tilt—always trains, subway
tracks he must cross, sewers
sloping, a difficult clamber

over the edge of a platform
as the twin beams emerge
at the end of the tunnel, grow
steady, bright, toward his fear:

The moon on the right means
you are left of the moon.
The moon on the left means
you are right of the moon.

Prayer Museum

Threshold from red to umber, blur
      from vein-blue to molten, a shudder
in the field of the outflung bedsheet—
      snaps taut. Or the black crease
between russet and rose that absorbs
      the restless gap. Sleepless,

she works herself up to the ratty edge
      of cease-to-be in the space of three
mental sentences—metastases, rattle,
      nothing—fear nightcap,
cruel cordial, spit spot. Nothing
      to watch except the vine tracing

its margin behind her eyes, red coils
      with licking blue flames inside.
Whose fear? Whose fate? What blaze?
      Nothing. But then the void
gulps down the noun of itself, coughs,
      offers up its tacky gift of hope—

one thought, not any of the thoughts that
      flank it: the morning after her death
her son would get up, put on the radio.

Museum of Incandescent Lighting

Remembers the girl in the ad—
　　　Saxoleine, Pétrole de Sûreté,
the restaurant redolent of lamp oil

　　　and ammonia vapors off the aged
cheese. L'Isle de St. Louis, the name
　　　of the place recalled:

L'Auberge de la Reine Blanche.
　　　She watches him lick
his fingers, touch the chimney

　　　of the hurricane lamp, flinch.
He removes the glass,
　　　sets it down on the table.

When the filament replaces
　　　the flame. When the wick
burns down to the dish. He

　　　licks his fingertips again,
pinches the flame to snuff it.
　　　He could not be more like his father.

Museum of Gems and Minerals

The guy working the night shift at the reception desk gets there at seven. Max starts hanging around at six, running his hands down the rail of the access ramp. They have been here longer than anywhere else—into the second week. A shaded sidewalk, a small fridge, a temp job with an air-conditioned office and the boss is mostly gone.

The clerk pulls his Rabbit into the reserved spot and winks at Max as he punches in. He is lanky, sunless pale, wearing a black T-shirt with the logo of an unknown band. His books all have orange "used" stickers on the bindings and he writes notes in them with a pen. He tells Max about black holes, kung fu, CPR, offers pointers on the uses of profanity, the gradations of significance from crud to crap to shit, frig to fuck, cow to cunt. The day after his day off he brings Max some specimens from his old rock collection. For keeps.

Claire comes down to retrieve Max at nine, finds them playing cards. She stands by the fan in her tank top and tries not to be too impatient to have him in bed, rolls the stiffness out of her shoulders.

When they get back to the room he boasts of new knowledge—there's a difference between a mineral and a rock. A mineral has its own crystals, but they are too small to see and are made of x-rays that originally came from other planets before they lost their light. A rock might have mud in it, or bits of plants and animals that have already died.

On Saturday afternoon she takes a late nap, the motel drapes darkening all but a blinding crack of sun. Max potters around, munches a handful of dry cereal. He likes this hotel. The toilet has a door but the sink is in the room with the bed.

He gets out his plastic magnifier and his specimens, which he keeps in a drawstring Crown Royal bag he found behind a wedding place in New Jersey. Quartz, turquoise, malachite, tourmaline, mica, pyrite, galena. He lines them up on the sink, polishes each stone with his breath and a washcloth, tries not to leave a print.

He is in the bathroom when there is a knock.

Claire sits up instantly, swings her legs over and checks the peephole. It is the clerk, hands in his pockets. She opens the door and he

shoulders his way in.

It's not him.

Sideburns, jersey. Not him. A man in a black jersey, knit cap. Shoves. She stumbles, pulls the night table between herself and

he grabs her purse, wedges a heavy shoe between the chair and an open

drawer. He grabs the cash on the bureau, ring, watch, dumps a bag, and another.

Of value.

A car alarm begins to bleat in the parking lot.

The man turns, ducks out.

The door clangs against the deadbolt.

She stands. Rights her skirt. Front in the front.

Starts to put things back in.

Starts to put things back in. Goes to the bathroom and tells Max to come out. The door is ajar. Come on, we're going. He doesn't look up.

Drags him out the door. In the breezeway, he stops to count his rocks again to be sure he has all seven, drops one on the steps—they are open concrete steps and it almost falls through the back but he gets it in time. She tugs him along, maneuvers him into the car.

No! he screams as she pulls around the drive, past reception, past the bougainvillea. You have to go back. You have to return the key.

Museum of the Alphabet

And a knick-knack paddy-whack, give.
One, two, buckle my shoe. Calico Jam,
the little fish swam, over the syllabub sea.
Calico Drum, the grasshoppers come
in the garden of Shut-Eye Town where
the fruit it bears is so good little monkey,
but always very curious. If you go flying
on a flying trapeze, said his mother, I will
become a tightrope walker and walk across
the air to you. Pepper and vinegar
are very good indeed, if only I had
a runcible spoon, some quince, some
honey and plenty of money, wrapped up
in a five-pound note. I won't. Just go
back to sleep. I won't. Tom put on
the tam-o-shanter, but it was too big
for him. Tiptoeing with solemn face
with some flowers and a vase. A sign
outside the door read visitors from 2–4.
The Vorpal blade went snicker-snack.
He left it dead. Peter who was very
naughty went straightaway. We'll
sell you the string that ties the key
to the king's garden. Goodbye thing,
you sing too long. Noises everywhere.

Sensation Museum

Thigh on vinyl,
she twists her
skirt down again,

straightens the seam.
He closes his eyes,
a shredded tissue

balled in his fist
as the car slides
sideways in silence

then crackles over
muddy gravel.
Nauseated, he

presses his cheek
on tempered glass.
Once she wrapped

a block in sandpaper
to smooth down
a splintered gash

in the floor. Cork.
Wool. Her hand
so dry from detergent

that the scratch
the child's nail made
on it was white

as chalk dust. She
gets out of the car,
finds some frozen

mulch, scrapes
bare handed and
scatters it behind

the tires on the icy
pavement so they
can drive away.

American Diner Museum

He watches the waitress watch his mother's body—
her hand still wrapped around the empty glass—gives her
another minute. He's finished, read the menu twice,

watched the booths fill up for breakfast, crumpled napkins
and johnnycakes, eggs Benedict, Madge with the carafe
stepping behind the blue-ribbon festoonery of the pie case

for a sheet of wax paper. The signs say Gumbo on Friday,
Help Wanted BUSS TEAM, baby back ribs, beef brisket,
butterscotch sundae, scalloped potatoes, pastrami on rye.

He tries to remember where they had the frog-eye salad
—tapioca and Funmallows—the Zuni Stew, the churros,
beans-and-chicharrones burritos—was it Swanky Frank's

with its lazy Susans of shortcake, the shanty on Wabash
with kale and spice, Hoosier chicken and Boston cream,
Formica that could be anywhere: cottage cheese, cukes,

Grape Nuts, pickle relish. A soda and a chaw of meat.
A map of names for cold cuts on a long loaf: hero,
hoagie, bomber, po'boy, zep, grinder, wedge. At first

it was anything he wanted and then it was *this is what
you get*. A restaurant once a day, then every other day,
then *wait until supper*—the car's in the Piggly Wiggly

parking lot, trunk half-full of groceries that won't spoil—
Ritz, Smuckers—a small propane stove to heat a can
of corn or Dinty Moore. He excuses himself, stands

in the center of the windowless bathroom mirrored
on four walls to infinity—back of the back of the back
of his head, smothering in the odor of ash and Pinesol.

When he comes back, she's still tracing a finger around
the rim of her water glass, rattling the last piece of ice.
The waitress rips the chit off the pad, circles the total.

House of Death

Late at night when she falls asleep
      before he does, he lies across
the foot of the bed and changes
      channels. Iron lung,
a girl clings to the doctor's coat
      as he closes the hatch,
a man screams *don't cut* as
      they wheel him out
of the ward, a mouthpiece dangles
      from an electric chair.
Patina must be a type of sore.
      Learns that bees like
meat better than sweets,
      that a half-girl, half-fish
can be gills and heels, that
      abature refers to traces
left by a stag in underbrush,
      abattoir comes from
French, for slaughterhouse.
      So that's the money shot:
eyelash strap leash lick lip-
      stick leg smear spur
grimace crease cringe cry.
      The later it gets the more
the words get snagged on one
      another—banana split,
Russian split, split lip. Schism,
      fiscal, chrysalis, malpractice.
Undertaker, understudy, under-
      stand, overhand, overcook,
overlook, overbear, bare-handed,
      bare-headed, beheaded.

Max's Dreamland II

He is the boy who could swallow the sea,
slurp the whole of it into his cheeks,
lips in a drawstring pucker, hold it all
while everyone he knows runs to gather

the fish that flop on the puddled sand.
No one heeds him as he starts to sway,
gestures wildly with his arms, reddening,
struggling—then the crush of foam, salt.

He wakes in a sweat, tries to think
about the time he and his dad built
a model trebuchet, medieval upgrade
of the catapult, lobbed golf balls

and acorns at the neighbor's fence. Or
the complex choreography of the self-
defense class: grab the attacker's foot,
twist the toe, pivot to strike the head.

Stasis swells, lies in wait—his limbs
fill with beans but his brain keeps on
pedalling and he can't get away from
the dog that follows along the fence,

its ham tongue hanging over blackened
gums—can't run from the baby goats,
bits of shit in the fur of their rears—can't
shake off the cockscomb brushing his hand.

Restaurant Mutiny

Women don't wander, they abandon.
They get up and walk right out of this
dingy joint at the end of a long wharf
while their kid's in the shop, poring over
the clippings and relics of some guy's
obsession with naval revolt, Clark Gable
with his chest hair, all seafaring bravado
and brass. Such as the Sharon, New
England whaler, which was subject to
mass desertions and several attempted
mutinies before it saw the murder
and dismemberment of its sociopathic
captain by four Polynesians pressed into
service. Or the Somers, where a trio
of unruly teens got hanged for acting up.
Spy glass. Sextant. Iron oar-lock
purportedly from the Amistad, not that
they ever got that far in history class.

She's had it up to here with his sass,
belligerence, backtalk, daily mopes—
nothing nothing nothing nothing nothing.
Eat some hush puppies and shut up.
Shut some posh hippies and eat sup.
Every shrug a prelude to open rebellion,
each eye-roll a strike against her power.

What a slut she once was, should be.
Mutineer, musketeer, mouseketeer—
the best part's when the boys swoon
for the townie chicks—a steamy liaison

in the Tiki hut but between her legs
is subterfuge. She too could bare a boob
but who would be her cohort, clan?
Whose command could she overthrow,
whose ship could she seize? Another
species of self-splitting. Wholesale
massacre, guerrilla tactics—garrisons
refuse to rescue the marooned loyalists
and the sea, of course, is indefatigable.

Gesundheit, Fletcher Christian, it looks
the same upside down: rank and file, men
with their high seas, their moby dicks,
opening their arms to make love to universal
freedom. He's in there, one of them. Man
in making, testing out his best swashbuckle,
impersonating ruthless will. Ready to arm.

All she has to do is start the car and drive
away, take her place among the monsters,
mothers who stripped duty off the stalk,
mute now, mute, eyes focused so far off
they might as well be fixed on open sea.

Liars Hall of Fame

Jackalope. Pinocchio. Nixon. Thank you for coming. We'd love to but we have a lot on our plate. Final closeout sale ends Saturday. You're the only one bothered by it. Satisfaction guaranteed. It's a perfect replica. All you need is love. When they put the baby in your arms, you will know what to do. You must change your life. You can change your life. He couldn't hurt a fly. The check's in the mail. He didn't see her the night of the murder. I can stop any time I want. This won't hurt a bit. All you need is a change of scenery. A change of heart. A change of clothes. Clothes make the man. Iago, with an asterisk—only insinuation. Münchausen. I won't come in your mouth. Love is all you need. Art matters. Thank you for coming. That wasn't so bad. All you need is a museum of clear ideas. The boy who cried wolf. Münchausen by proxy. No interest, no money down. We have your best interests at heart. He didn't lay a hand on her. Peter, three times before the cock crowed. The worst is over. I'm so glad you came. It will go away on its own. When he's grown he won't even remember.

Pharmacy Museum

Claire tells the woman she needs something for the sleeplessness, something that won't dull her vigilance, her reaction to alarm. The woman behind the counter looks at her, neither shakes her head nor nods.

She is a plum-skinned black woman in a voluminous dress, her hair wrapped so tightly in a gold scarf that her temples are pulled taut. In the half-second before she can check herself, Claire looks around for the woman's boss.

The woman's gaze sets her straight. She is impassive, invincible as a pope. Her eyes, set deeply over ashen pouches of flesh, execute their steady intake of evidence, analysis. It is her shop. Proprietor, stock clerk, insurance claim processor, all. And healer—the license to dispense and advise is right there on the wall.

Claire steps back outside and looks around for Max, who has promised to follow in a minute. The store is a freestanding clapboard structure in a red-dirt parking lot, next to a gas station where the pumps aren't electronic but the old half-digit flip dials. The building has a covered porch with a Coca-Cola cooler, a defunct payphone, and a placard: Museum Hours 10 to 4.

Several boys and a girl in overalls are playing on the porch and in the yard. When Max comes up the steps all of them draw back and sit up on the rails. One boy props his feet on the arm of a rocker, pushing it back and forth over the slats. In the corner there's a broken baby doll—twig at the neck where the head was once attached, a dimple in its plastic tush.

Claire rubs her eyes. It's been several days since she's slept more than a few hours. The headless baby seems to roll. Baby with a brainstem, baby with a seamless crotch. Hush, baby.

God help her, any remedy will do, home or otherwise. God help Dewey Dell when she walked into a store just like this and asked for a remedy to her predicament, a store where she was offered—took—the hair of the dog. Hush-a-bye, Dewey Dell, there's no difference now, not for decades, not for dollars, not for the lotto machine in the corner and the Medicaid enrollment forms on the bulletin board. Even then ten dollars in your bra couldn't get you an abortion or a ticket out, not a ticket far enough from anywhere to matter.

Inside, the room is dustless, ordered down to the baseboards. Along one wall are rows of amber-glass bottles and jars, labeled at intervals in typewriter Courier: digestive tonics, mineral oils, antiseptics. It is hard to tell where the shop ends and the museum begins. Vitamins, Alka-Seltzer, Cold-EEZE. Powders the color of goldenrod, turmeric. Green-glass pints with cloudy rosettes in relief around the label. Wide-mouthed beakers with their bases wrapped in tin.

Above them, in plain wooden frames, are portraits: women in their best hats, men vested and suited, men in fragile spectacles, aunts and cousins, a father before he left for the war. There are a few ledges with precisely placed artifacts—enamel cups, shell casings, dog tags. Above the cash register, the woman's mother's mother's mother—an opaque face, stolid will.

Mom, come on. Her pink-beige son, tugging her sleeve. Her pink-beige son—destined to move swiftly through the airport queue, to avoid getting pegged a troublemaker by the principal, to be assumed studious when he's staring at his hands. Assumed to be official, as Dewey Dell assumed a young white man would be when she walked into that pharmacy, found the young white man standing at his post.

The hair of the dog that bit you, Dewey Dell. What made you bend over for the pimpled clerk—ignorance, desperation, desire? When what you needed was the pharmakon—the poison and the antidote. When what you needed was *rue*, known for its abortifacient properties if the dose is high enough. A woman could walk in. A woman could catch a break. A man, stone-drunk, could as a stunt smash the amber bottle on his skull and not get bloodied.

She stops herself. She is not Dewey Dell. This is not the post-Reconstruction South. This is the world long after Lincoln, long after Selma, Kent, Till, King. The world of Obama after all—the day after whose election she went through the McDonald's drive-thru and rejoiced with the black cashier on their better world. Then took her change and drove away.

The woman pushes a packet of tablets across the counter—the straight bones of her hand pronounced beneath her skin. Claire tucks it in her purse. Take with a full glass of water. Valerian, hyoscyamus niger. Take it easy. Natrum muriaticum, Hepar sulph, belladonna, castor oil. Is that how it is? White Woman pays a call to the Magic Dark Woman once again? Demands a potion for Fast Luck: cinnamon, bergamot, verbena.

Max groans, leans on the door, kicks back a ball that's been kicked to him. Carry on, citizen. Come on out here and carry on. What are you, some kind of ninny? Does she hear it? The word whitey or redneck or cracker? Does she hear it in her own head? The ball goes over the balustraded porch and someone belts out a Boyz-II-Men refrain, vaults over the hedge.

Her boy, wiry and mad. Glowering at her in his livid embarrassment.

Here, Dewey Dell, throw a rope over the lintel. Throw yourself a lifeline. Watch it coil into a noose. Is that you, Dewey Dell? Is that your mind, your speechless mind, that threw that rope over the lintel? Is that your mind that made that noose?

Carhenge

Waking on the equinox with her chin
on the armrest and knees wedged under
the steering wheel. He still fits across

the backseat. Smoke hangs in the east
where the substation caught fire the night
before, somewhere on a dull stretch

of US 385 beyond Alliance, some
distance from destitution but headed
toward the white cinderblock wall

of a sandpit amphitheatre where the sun
rises, pries the night open between
warped hoods of Caddies, pick-ups

all painted gray, all aligned upright
to testify to, flout the force of a magnet
strong enough to lift a car on end.

Home Sweet Home Museum

They circle back toward the northeast, stop short of the Mason-Dixon line. A mere 250 miles from

home. Not back, not going back. She stops in Gambrills, Maryland, the town where she grew up, where she knows

no one. Parents long since moved away, downsized to a condo, then dead within a year of each other.

She half expects to find Nana Flynn still sitting on the screened-in porch watching Merv. But no one is on the street or any of the others she turns down to get there. Too hot to be outside, locust-hiss August haze.

Some kind of Ithaca. The sign on the corner says Soccer Camp at the Rec Council and she knows the park, knows her son's face is bewildered and bone-tired with loneliness. She borrows some shin guards from another mom, writes a check that is probably bad.

And she's free until three o'clock. She parks the car on her old street and starts walking, past the house where she practiced for dance-team tryouts, past where the German Shepherd jumped on her on the way home from second grade. She can still feel its claws on the back of her nylon parka. Past the house where she lost her virginity to Michael Towle's best friend, or tried to, in the den where he put "Misty" on the stereo and failed for nerves. The next time he managed it. Endless subdivision,

split foyers close together, concrete stoops, aluminum siding and geraniums. Michael Towle was the one she had wanted—tawny and broad-shouldered, practicing the double bass with his shirt off. A mailbox with a flip-flop motif, Garfield in the back of a sedan. A couple of girls are staging a stuffed-animal sale but there is no one to buy. Then, abruptly, the neighborhood gives out onto the rural road past the dairy farm, the long straightaway where Mr. O'Dell taught them all to do U-turns, where Jason Tate played chicken with Jeff Kenyon and lost, killed in the head-on collision from which Jeff walked away. The tiny intersection with the state road makes it a town: post office, Dr. Patel's sloping Victorian, Jerman's Feed & Grain. She wonders if they still sell chicks, stacked by breed in aluminum racks.

She turns back. She has no water and there is no shade. In 1987, the year she was a high school sophomore, Sherri Walczak's mother was raped and murdered while out jogging in these fields in the early morning. There were apocryphal accounts of a satanic heart excision. She heard later that a cold-case squad had linked the crime to a man already in prison.

She makes it back to the house, now shuttered a different color. Occupants at work, the yard maintained, the front door upgraded with a stained-glass oval. Some broken rattan ready to go out to the curb.

A hello from across the street. Not Nana but Missy Flynn, all grown up. Hair permed, smoker's cough. She remembers Claire, who used to babysit her. Tells her that her sister Jenny joined the police force in Gaithersburg.

A ringing in her ears, a surge of queasy-headedness, sweat. Some thickened Ithaca. An onslaught she knows—even as she knows she might grow dizzier and fall—is only the overaccumulation of proper names. Forsaken for a fool's ransom, a remedy, a song. All the home-grown revolts put down, rolled under sod. Nothing left except a drifter's history, a mutiny gallery. Jenny Flynn packs heat.

She could stay here. She and Max could rent a duplex with new vinyl siding.

She gets herself to the park with a bottle of water, waits for the digital minutes: 2:52, 59. When he gets in the car, she maneuvers to the interstate and drives west faster than the law allows.

Wheels Through Time Museum

97,556 and counting
rosaries by tens on her knuckles or the grips of the steering wheel,
    making her way through
the Hail Mary's and Glory Be's, the decades of sorrowful mysteries
    she can't remember
beyond the business of carrying, falling with, being nailed to
    a cross, steering around
potholes and roadkills, every night expecting an agent of the law
    to appear at the door
but what charge would he level—truancy? unseemly love? overlove?
    She'll road-school him
in asters, lupine, goldenrod, gullies, mesas, badlands, petrified forests,
    pick up curricula
for the state tests in the next town and be on her way, thank you for asking.
    She knows the oil's
still ample on the dip stick, God bless her Honda, keeps her eyes on the
    odometer not calendar—
98,003, upshifting to the joyful mysteries, unable to recall a single one
    beyond the virgin birth,
beyond the next tenth, next mile. She keeps both hands on the wheel—
    moves on to the luminous,
the episode where Jesus leaves his friends and burns up on re-entry—
    99,200, lighting out
for the territory, for the far horizon, for the TNT-blasted valley, muscling
    through the freeway snarl,
the cloverleaf, hitting the Pacific and swinging north to follow the coast
    and on up the spine,
the fault. She turns to him: let's flip it and start again from zero.

Paperweight Museum

The girl goes walking in the city
and the storm begins, snow settling
on garlanded façades, taxicabs,
her coat. A world full of water
with a teaspoon of air at the top.
Bubbles blown in with syringes
while glass is still molten, a knife
plunged into multi-colored sand.

She has a bunny tail and bustier,
Tweety Bird eyes. If you shake her,
she disrobes; when the sediment
settles, the catsuit's on again. She
lives in a place where there are no
cypress trees, no Roman ramparts.
Interior figures are acrylic, lit
from a bulb in the melamine base.

The girl stays in bed long after
the lover has left. Props herself
against the cheap veneer. Lamps
are brass and bolted down, curtains
drawn with a cord on a pulley
that swings free. In the last gasp,
the lover looked away from her
flesh, as from a needle stick.

The girl is getting up now, opens
the window. Papers blow across
the bureau—map, take-out menu,
missive to herself on waking. Heavy

odor of workshirt, menthol cigarettes.
She looks around for something to
hold it all down—lead-crystal apple,
bronzed baby shoes, a rock from

the grave of Elvis. Just not a globe,
please not a globe, a little world.

American Precision Museum

Now what—should she head Thelma-style off
a cliff with her kid in the car? Should there come

a day when she can't shake dawn's despair
before they break camp along the drywash,

and drives for several days across shorn tableland,
stopping when the sun relents to walk the ocean

floor, the lime deposits of ancient brachiopods
sifting through her hands? At this rate it's not

long before the hills rise again, older and more
solemn than before. On the slope up ahead

a square of forest has been cut away, a patch
of fur shaved off a dog for surgery. She is tired.

Paid it all: tuition, dues, tolls. Where the hell's
the *deus ex machina*? There's still the matter

of the inevitable split, the centripetal fact
in store for this pair: the time available to orbit

each other in this irregular ellipse, quaint egg
with a wobble, must soon come to an end. Invention

of interchangeable parts "on a practical level"
has to happen for the Etheric Force Main Stator

to exist: he could grow up to be both machinist
and artist, assemble his wares in a former armory

and wait for her to give approval, which she already
has, but such doublings are rare. Her own future

depends on understanding the inbuilt difficulty,
the impasse—the typewriter, *s* far from *o*,

m far from *e*, the strained chiasmus intended to
slow the strokes, prevent jams. Soon overcome.

Expedience corrupts design. Flight comprises risk,
the chaotic tedium of a choose-your-own ending:

a) flea market; b) beauty school; c) quicksand.
He starts to read instructions for the Windsor gun.

She counts the cash—takes one more vicious swipe
of the credit card long since overdrawn, curses her

useless MFA. Now that she's ripped herself out
of the safety nets, what if he falls, what if she feels

a lump in her breast? She could kick herself for
setting up some story that's going to have to end

with the riff and ripstop of a frantic, cacophonous
coda and a wail of jazz horns—mutes in, mourning.

Liquid Paper Museum

Homebrew perfected by Bette Nesmith, mom
of ex-Monkee Michael Nesmith, in a trailer

behind her Dallas home, until she made enough
to move the plant to Nambe. American redemption:

IBM declined to buy, but after making it herself
for 17 years, she sold it to Gillette for 47 million.

Ordinary difficulties, names like a string
of Christmas lights in an RV park, portable

generators for blue-lit interiors, broadcasting
the *Wheel of Fortune* theme. A privy nearby

emits its fetor of liver and garlic. It's late.
He's been asleep beside her for hours

and the toddler face has surfaced, erased
the sullen, nervy, pre-teen scowl. Fetal deep,

arms crossed, fingers curled. Takes him
in her arms. Thinks, I may be falling asleep,

I may actually be falling asleep if I can stop
thinking about falling asleep, if I can draw

a shade down on this mind, stand alone
by a creek beneath oak-addled light, alone

in a night garden, a caryatid with an urn—
she feels her mind slip, finds herself among

the standees on a packed bus, then the bus
becomes a coldroom, fogged with breath,

their bodies strung up like sides of beef.

The End Is Near Museum

Adopt-a-Highway: Daughters of the American Revolution of Bethlehem.
She parks at a Mobil minimart a few hilly miles east of the interstate,
a stretch where tony burbs fade into farmland and distribution hubs,
petrochemical plants and paper mills. He'll never find us if we keep moving.
Adopt-a-Highway: Haverstraw Wrestling Boosters. Another river swollen
over its banks, a broad yellow stillness that a fast-moving piece of trash
belies. Transaction denied. Signs in the median: foreclosure sale, furniture
close-out. Local agent dispatched. Adopt-a-Highway: AA of Odenton and
True-Value Hardware. She carried the boy across state lines. Adopt-a-
Highway: Pecan Alliance. The earth dropping away below the trestle bridge.
Adopt-a-Highway: La Petite Academy Daycare. A slip of paper, creased
twice. Adopt-a-Highway: Jericho Redemption Hall of Okeechobee. One last
thin disc of Lifesaver before he can't stand it anymore and lets it give way to
the teeth. Promises, promises. Power lines, up ahead on the plateau.

Museum of Papermaking

Rita rents out 2R, lives in 2F above
her store, a copy shop with sundries, fax.

Filipina or Latina or Sicilian-Lebanese.
New Jersey, she answers, Freehold.

She fans a ream, taps it deftly into
the drawer, notices Max watching.

Gestures him around the counter—
want to see where I make paper?

Backroom with a vat, burner, planks
leaning against an old-style Frigidaire.

Basic frame, mold and deckle, stretched
with nylon netting, stapled perimeter.

A *Twinrocker*, varnished smooth.
She tells him how she makes pulp

in a plastic dishpan, one-inch squares
soaked and then run through a blender—

methods of Dixie Junius. Papyrus to rag
to hemp to mulberry to groundwood to

chemical pulp. Crash course. Upstairs,
vacant 2R has a tub in the kitchen,

a water closet so small his knees bump
the wall, three windows and an alcove

with a sliding door. Rita shrugs. Stay
a week, a month, a year, see if I care.

Museum of Museums

Never made it to the Museum of Magic, the World of Rubber, the Barbie
Hall of Fame, the Museum of Holography, or the 24 Hour Church of Elvis.
Never saw the Hall of Also-Rans, the Creation Evidences Museum, the
Stolen Bell Museum, or Bruce's Whoop-n-Holler. Skipped the WHAMKA—
Williams Hall Art Museum of Kitsch Art—for obvious reasons. No use
for decoys, antique motors, nitroglycerin, UFOs, King Tut, or Laura
Ingalls Wilder. No Peace Museum, no Harmony Harmony Museum, no
International Mother's Day Shrine. No Conspiracy Museum either. Turns to
her: Mom, where's the Louvre?

Honey of a Museum

She goes out alone, wanders the stalls of a Saturday market.

Hive box, antique smoker, lore of the queen. The honey vendor sees her looking and holds out a jar, an amber orb with a comb. The gesture gives her a jolt—

a man's hand, broad, clean-nailed. The hand of man who might unfold her arm and kiss the soft fossa where blood is drawn.

There she goes, weak in the bee's knees. The cat's pajamas. Not wearing pajamas. Bees in her bonnet. Minding her own beeswax. Spelling, quilting, sting like a. Make a beeline. Be mine, be mine. She shakes her head, tries to compose

her face into a normal shopper's expression when

a girl approaches the stand. No more than fourteen—gamine, black eyeliner and Chucks. She picks up a honey jar and it slips out of her hand onto the asphalt. Aghast,

the girl stoops to grab the pieces, stands up with a gash. A spurt.

The honey man steps around the table, takes the girl's hand between his thumb and finger, holds firm. I'm bleeding, she yelps. He looks at Claire. I have a first-aid kit in the car, if you could just stand here and hold pressure. Claire takes the hand from him, as if given

a small animal with claws, presses her thumb over the cut as he has done. The girl squirms, lets out a sob. She is trying hard not to look at the cut or at Claire, who adjusts her grip, feels their two pulses syncopate beneath the touch, feels their pulses rise through the market din, the roar from the thruway overpass, the fear muffled inside her head—a gust in a duct—the girl's life slipping away

in her hands. But it is only a mishap. The honey man comes back with an EMT, gauze, mop. The girl's mother is called. A joke is made. No one is unduly alarmed.

First National Church of the Exquisite Panic

Where on earth could he have gone?
     Chews her cuticle, thinks
about the chapel of *pharblongence,*
     Yiddish for total confusion,
laughter, art, and the road to Nevada.
     Thinks a whole buncha nonsense
about taking off her clothes and painting
     her body cerise while the company
mocks up the set to look like blood
     fondue, a *trompe l'oeil* of urban
ravenous decay, a crack-up, architected
     destruction, *isn't that funny!*
So where is he. Rita hasn't seen him

     since they came back after lunch.
Try the arcade. The underpass, the drum
     of the stormdrain, new rocks spread
in their culvert. Pool under construction,
     empty. Where the hell could he
have gone? She checks the car again.
     Sits down. Makes herself a cocktail
of panic—shaken, not stirred. Enough time
     has passed that this should be over,

isn't. Remembers the toddler lost in T. J. Maxx,
     turning up in the clearance rack
between corduroy and lamé. Scanning for
     his red shirt in the field trip crowd
coming around the henhouse. Another time
     a little worse: no boy came down
the school bus steps, the monitor shrugged.

This time what explanation,
what revelation of fault? God help him
if she. God help her if he.

Prayer Museum II

Forehead to the ground,
she wills the prayer to work
the way sound works,

detonation and flash, pulse
here here here here here
as the sound moves

through its substance:
wall   body   water   each
molecule pushed by

the wave into the next,
pushed through, pushing
the stuff out of the way,

pushing the hearer out
of its way, willing him
to get his ass back here.

She petitions the tile,
the grout between
tiles, implores the air

conditioner, a toggle-
bolt beside the vent,
begs the bitten flesh

inside her cheek
to yield, bleed, begs
the thunder, the sheet

of rain that comes with
the egregious menace
of this sallow sky.

The Lightning Field

Outside the town of Quemado
—*burned*—he faces west
to watch the valley smolder,

stretches his sweatshirt over
his knees. *Elemental Hero*
Wingman initiates the duel,

summons Archfiend and
Pandemonium, otherwise
he will negate the Tribute

and the attack is unbearable.
Four hundred stainless
steel rods set in a plane,

each one high as a house.
The storm ignites itself,
voltage stitchery, until

the entire sky goes white
between waves of down-
pour, the earth gouged out

in light, in spades. *Wing-*
man, Avian, Wildheart,
why not remember, why

not reply, when fear can be
fathomed, summoned up
by suns to double the power?

When the storm is over, black.
He could find his way back by
moonlight but there is none.

Max's Dreamland III

His father sinks sure as Jesus through
the leafy canopy, so he has to believe
harder to make him rise and walk across
the treetops, born aloft on fronds, above

the gnarled overgrowth, out of reach
of monkey and macaw—across an open
field, blind glare from a bare-bulb sun,
until a fuse whips itself out and the nova

explodes, nothing but a flash, no man.

He hits the ground and breaks into a run:
humid darkness in his own throat, moss
giving way beneath his feet, a long skid
in the mud as he almost falls, hurdles

a knee into spongy earth, and he can't
lift it again, can't run, can't lift or lift or
lift his head, cheek on the dirt—imprint,
rune, tattoo—*hey Jude hey Jude hey Jude.*

Experimental Breeder Reactor #1

In the first blue, with only Orion left in the last
phosphorus cells of dark, the darkness of interiors
with static-snow screens after broadcasts cease,
the dark of nuclei where unstrung beads diverge
to release the fire that binds them, dividing
zygotes emerging from their exponential rise
to the next power, to the next and next, rising
over the bluff beyond the billboard, beyond
the bare filament that brightens to burn a line
inside the closed eye, beyond the rows of rods
that hang the wires that transmit the current
to the twinning circuits of this mid-sized city
that's waking now, moving close enough now
to light the fuse that detonates the day—his face.
You look like a drowned rat is all she can say.

Next-to-Last Museum

Here's hoping: a gust through the open
window lifts the newsprint off the table

and it slides, exposes a buxom swimmer
in a travel ad spanning the centerfold,

catching her son's eye as he eats his cereal,
the contour of a man's shoulders bent

over the bowl—a ripple in the foliage
that suggests the granite ridge—the page

slipping to the floor, forming a flimsy tent
on the linoleum. She reaches to pick it up—

paper trail, paper doll, paper cut, paper
clip, paper money—all the evidence

of movement, maneuvers, catching up
with her at last, at the table, in a morning

full of rigged ballots, conspiracy theories,
tainted vaccines, unemployment, a breeze

lifting the newsprint while the clock ticks
the last ten minutes she has before she has

to leave for work, to leave this shabby flat
full of paper—brown, butcher, wrapping,

graph, toilet, construction, tracing, wall—
envelopes of several sizes, paper airplanes,

funny papers, pads—not a pink slip,
not a lot of cash, just the honey man's

number on a scrap in her purse, a want
ad from the local rag, an obsolete list,

a tattered card, and across the table—
her son, lifting a bowl to drink. She

lets the breeze pick up the page again,
weights it down with her free hand.

Fall River House of Law & Disorder

Double knock. She glimpses a navy blur
through the smudged pane, zooms in:
the crease of a standard-issue trouser.

No choice but to open—stout policeman
on the porch, framed in full sun. Her
eye goes straight to the service revolver.

Tilt and whirl, the floorboards pitch
as the gaze swings up and out, a hop-
skip from the curbside ginkgo to

the blue Pine Bluff water tower to
the low gray line that is a bit of river.
Make a run for it. As seen through

the doorframe, his upright body
blocks the metal shaft and base
of the utility pole so its tines

emerge from his head. Balding.
No sacrificial mesa, no glacier, no
pyre. She looks down at his hands—

fur and knuckle—wonders why
men seldom expose their wrists,
why the world elapses, collapses

between cufflink and handcuff.
He produces a ballpoint pen. She
steadies her gaze to it; he indicates

a warrant. Without lawful excuse.
By force or fraud. Turn yourself in
to the Teton Valley Doll Hospital

for willful refusal, happy lies, she
surmises, capsizes, since she did not
give what's due, did not duly notify.

Lift yourself up, latter-day Lazarus
of the Muscle Car Ranch—let violins,
violence, rise. You will be given

an opportunity to produce the child.
Redress the rebuke. Get yourself
to the Ave Maria Grotto, the last

theatrical lullaby, and if said child,
being competent, agrees, you might
exercise your right, retain. Put it

down to ignorance. Put it down
to pride. Put down the riot, the dog,
roots. Put this down: He might have.

Would have. Was capable of. No
last chance to ransom, reconcile, cure.
Make a break. She senses her solid

self rehearse the sinewed lift—knee,
thigh, hip—feels the first step quicken
over the threshold, the jamb, a half-

choked impulse of ardor, of ire,
as the body urges flight, as it yields
to the coming threat not with fear

but a form of motion—a gesture held
in check as she stands in the doorway,
collects herself, puts her foot down.

Notes

Many details for the museum settings in this book have been culled from *Little Museums: Over 1000 Small (and Not-So-Small) American Showplaces*, by Lynne Arany and Archie Hobson (Henry Holt, 1998). Facts and names have been altered to serve the journey of the characters, and neither geography nor weather corresponds to actual time or place. This is a work of poetic fiction. The people, events, circumstances, and institutions depicted in this book are fictitious or used fictitiously. Any resemblance to real persons, living or dead, is purely coincidental.

"Church of One Tree" cites the line "a perfect skepticism questions disbelief" from an interview with Alice Fulton by Cristanne Miller in *Contemporary Literature* 38.4 (1997), and draws on William James's arguments in "The Will to Believe": "faith based on desire is certainly a lawful and possibly an indispensable thing."

Italicized phrases in "Hello Gorgeous Hair Museum" are from Vladimir Nabokov's *Lolita* (1955).

"Musée Mécanique" refers to Francis Picabia's *L'Enfant Carburateur* (1919), mixed media on plywood. This poem is for James.

"American Diner Museum" draws some details from *Roadfood* by Jane and Michael Stern (HarperCollins, 1992).

"Pharmacy Museum" responds to Whitfield Lovell, *Restoreth* (2001), *Twine* (2001), and *The Day Before Yesterday* (2001), mixed media and found objects on wood, and also to William Faulkner's *As I Lay Dying* (1930).

"First National Church of the Exquisite Panic" refers to the religion founded by performance artist Robert Delford Brown. *Pharblongence* is an Anglicized form of the Yiddish *farblonjet*.

Italicized passages in "The Lightning Field" adapt some words and phrases from the card game Yu-Gi-Oh!

"Fall River House of Law & Disorder" echoes Bruce Nauman's *Violins Violence Silence* (1981–82), illuminated glass tubing.

About the Author

B. K. Fischer holds degrees in writing from Johns Hopkins and Columbia Universities, and a PhD in English and American Literature from New York University. She is the author of a critical study, *Museum Mediations: Reframing Ekphrasis in Contemporary American Poetry*, and her poems have appeared in *The Paris Review, Boston Review, The Hopkins Review, FIELD, Southwest Review, Crab Orchard Review, Literary Mama*, and other journals. She lives in Sleepy Hollow, New York, with her husband and three children.